THINK ~ON THESE~ THINGS

ATTITUDES FOR SUCCESSFUL LIVING

RAY BENTLEY

Think On These Things
Second Edition

by Ray Bentley

Published by

⛰ MARANATHAPRESS

© 1996, 2017 Ray Bentley
All rights reserved.

Printed in the United States of America
ISBN: 978-1-60039-356-3

For information, write to:

MARANATHA PRESS
10752 Coastwood Road, San Diego, CA. 92127.

Cover and Interior Layout: Brett Burner, Lamp Post

CONTENTS

INTRODUCTION

"Finally, whatever things are true, whatever things are noble, whatever things are pure, whatever things are lovely, whatever things are of good report, if there is any virtue and if there is anything praiseworthy – think on these things."

Philippians 4:8

Paul, the great apostle and writer of this letter, was more than a "think good thoughts" advocate. The words he penned to the church at Philippi did not come easily. They were born through years of suffering, doubts, confusion, striving, wrestling with right and wrong, and honest struggling to know the meaning of it all. Notice that he opens these thoughts with the word "finally."

That's because what precedes this paragraph is what made it possible for him to write it.

Paul was a successful man by the world's account. Educated, well-born and respected as a Jewish Roman citizen, he had the best of the secular and religious world.

Then he met the Lord Jesus Christ on the road to Damascus. All that well-bred success meant little to him in light of the truth and experience he encountered. Thirty years after his conversion, Paul sat in a Roman prison and poured his heart into a letter to his beloved church in Philippi. He reminded his friends that there had been difficult and painful times, and yes, there had been a price to pay for his devotion to Christ. But he had discovered the *secret of life*: **"For me to live is Christ."**

He closes his letter by giving a profound statement of what our attitude toward life should and can be – what will enable us to truly live a victorious life. "Rejoice in the Lord always! " he said. "Be anxious for nothing . . . and the peace of God, which surpasses all understanding, will guard your hearts and minds through Christ Jesus."

Finally, Paul says, with the peace of God guarding our hearts and minds, here is the key to God-inspired living: "Whatever things are true, whatever things are noble, whatever things are lovely, whatever things are of good report, if there is any virtue and if there is anything praiseworthy – think upon these things."

When my kids were young and things got out of control – yelling, wrestling, arguing, carrying on the way kids do – I'd stop everything with, "OK! It's time for an attitude check!"

Attitude is the way you think about someone or some situation. It's what is in your heart and mind, and influences how you behave.

Throughout Scripture we meet people who needed an "attitude check" – and adjustment. Peter certainly did, when in fear he denied Christ. Jonah did, when he struggled with obedience and a bad attitude toward God's plans for Ninevah.

All of us need an attitude check on occasion. Pastor Chuck Swindoll says, "I believe the single most significant decision I can make on a day-to-day basis is my choice of attitude."

After Paul taught us what things we should "think upon," he summed up his thoughts with this astounding statement: "I can do all things through Christ who strengthens me" (Philippians 4:13).

All things . . . that's pretty amazing, when you think about it. My prayer is that through this book, you will explore various aspects of your life, checking your attitude and making adjustments. No matter how hard, painful, puzzling or extreme our circumstances, we can indeed do "all things through Christ"!

CHAPTER ONE

GOD

Godly Attitudes Start With God

Life falls into place only with God.

Our attitude toward life begins with our attitude toward God. That depends greatly on how we perceive Him; who we believe He is; what we believe He means to our lives; what our understanding of Him is.

H.G. Wells once wrote, "Until a man has found God and been found by God, he begins at no beginning, he works to no end. He may have his friendships, his partial loyalties, his scraps of honor. But all these things fall into place, and life falls into place, only with God."

Wells was not known as a particularly devout man, but he had grasped an important truth.

For most of us, our perception of God is all tied up in religious thoughts and institutions. For some, God is a force of nature, an ethereal unreal being. For others, God is a concept, to be bent according to our whims and hopes. For many, God is a very real person with Whom we have a relationship.

That's where I'd like to begin: Defining our relationship with God.

A VERY RELIGIOUS MAN

"I've gone to church all my life," the woman cried to her counselor. "I've tried to be a good wife and mother, but . . . ." She kneaded the tissue in her hands nervously. She showed no inclination to stop the tears that poured from her eyes.

"He," referring to her husband, "ushers in church. We go to an adult Sunday School class . . . but now he's not happy. Life is boring, he says. He needs more, wants more . . . I can't seem to give it to him. I don't know what it all means. Our religion doesn't seem to have any answers anymore."

People are often shocked when they believe their religion has failed them. Americans, especially, consider themselves to be a very religious people. Many Americans own at least one Bible, and many still believe the Bible is the written Word of God and is totally accurate in all that it teaches, although that number is diminishing.

This same majority puts religion at a place of high importance in their lives. However, this group admits to seldom actually reading the Bible.[1]

People are disillusioned with institutions, with the decaying nature of society, and the break down of families and morals. So, we are turning to religion in droves. But when we discover, as the woman above did, that "religion" doesn't have all the answers to our problems, it can be harshly disappointing.

Religion is not necessarily a good thing. It's not necessarily a bad thing, but it just isn't enough, as Jesus pointed out one night to a very religious man.

Nicodemus was a prominent Jewish ruler, whom we can read about in John chapter three. He was also a Pharisee and a theologian. As a religious leader, he taught others the laws of God, and observed them himself scrupulously. He tithed faithfully, he fasted, he prayed in the Temple, he set a good example to his people. He was a model church member!

But was he happy? A hunger still gnawed away at him, a feeling of discontent he couldn't quite satisfy with all his good deeds and religious service.

Late one night, under the cover of darkness, he sought out Jesus of Nazareth, a somewhat controversial itinerant preacher of his time.

---

1   George Barna, *The Barna Report*, (Regal Books, Ventura, California), 1992.

"Rabbi," Nicodemus addressed Him, "we know that You are a teacher come from God; for no one can do the things You do unless God is with him."

Nicodemus respected Jesus, and had drawn certain conclusions about Him. He acknowledged Him as a good teacher, and even as someone capable of miracles.

A SECOND BIRTH

Just a few verses above this story, the Bible says of Jesus that "He knew all men, and had no need that anyone should testify of man, for He knew what was in man" (John 2:25). Jesus knew what was in Nicodemus' heart. He didn't waste any time with philosophical discussions or polite conversation. He got right to the point: **"Most assuredly, I say to you, unless one is born again, he cannot see the kingdom of God."**

This is the first time in recorded history that the phrase "born again" is used in this way. It's a phrase that has been dragged through the media in recent years, maligned, made fun of, and often completely misunderstood. It even left Nicodemus, the theologian, baffled. He somewhat satirically asked Jesus, "How can a man be born when he is old? Can he enter a second time into his mother's womb and be born?"

So Jesus explained it to him this way: "That which is born of the flesh is flesh, and that which is born of the

Spirit is spirit. Do not marvel that I said to you, 'You must be born again.'"

Nicodemus' mind must have been reeling as he tried to think this through. With all his knowledge and intellectual prowess, he was still no doubt wondering to himself, *What does this have to do with me?* as he blurted out, "How can these things be?"

Jesus gently chided him, saying, "Are you the teacher of Israel, and do not know these things?"

In other words, you can be a very religious person, well-versed in religious philosophy and knowledge – maybe even a leader in your church or temple. Yet with all those credentials, you can still be ignorant of the one essential condition stipulated by Jesus for entering the Kingdom of God.

It's so logical, when you think about how Jesus explained it. "That which is born of flesh is flesh."

There are over seven billion people on this planet, and we all got here one way – and one way only. We were all born "of the flesh." Each of us came from our mother's womb.

But there is another spiritual, invisible world, which is all around us. It is inhabited by spiritual beings, like angels, and it is where the Kingdom of God resides. There is only one way to enter into this world as well. "That which is born of the Spirit is spirit." You must be spiritually born into it. You must be born again, by the Spirit of God.

The Spirit is like the wind, Jesus explained. We cannot physically see the Spirit of God. But just as we "see" the wind blowing in tree tops and feel its breeze upon our face, we can feel and see the effects of God's Spirit in our lives. Nicodemus, Jesus is saying, wake up! Being religious isn't enough. Whatever it is that's frustrating you, whatever it is that drove you to seek Me, whatever changes you need to make in your life, they must come by the Spirit of God.

Jesus met Nicodemus face to face. He challenged his mind and his intellect. Now He gets to the heart of the matter, found in that familiar verse, John 3:16:

"For God so loved the world that He gave His only begotten Son, that whoever believes in Him should not perish but have everlasting life."

That's what it means to be born again. By the Holy Spirit of God, we have the opportunity to pass from death to life. We are no longer bound by this world and its constraints. We will not perish. Our sin, our pain, our misery, the heartaches and failures that torment us and taunt us are now subject to a new order, to a new, eternal, life in the Kingdom of God.

THE BIG "DO OVER"

There's a scene in a Billy Crystal movie where he and his buddies are riding horses out on the range, completely out of their element, trying to figure out what life is all about. Billy Crystal, suddenly enlightened, says, "I know! Life is a do over!"

A "do over" is like when we were kids, he explains, and we messed up – and our parents said, "That's okay. You can do it over."

That's a reassuring thought to a kid – and for adults. Unfortunately, life's "mess-ups" get bigger and more complicated as we grow up. The stakes get higher, and in desperation, we keep hoping for a chance at a "do over."

Sometimes it feels like – if we could just get a new house . . . or job . . . or wife . . . or husband . . . then all our problems would be solved.

Or maybe a better self-help program is what's needed. A plan. A new set of resolutions! Promises to lose weight, be more patient, work harder, work less, etc. Haven't we all done that before?

The truth is, doing ourselves over is a tough, nearly impossible project – but not impossible, when God is doing the "do over," because with God, the Bible tells us, "all things are possible." But God's "do over" begins at the very core of our existence, our spiritual natures.

We get a chance at a "do over" the moment we are born again.

From the moment we are physically born, God's Spirit is *with* us, ministering to us. That is why we are so very aware of Him. Most people have a religious understanding, and even an historical acceptance of His existence. But believing in Him is a different matter, as Jesus wanted Nicodemus to understand. Believing means to trust Him to save you; to know that He died on the cross for you personally, and that He rose from the dead so that you too might be raised up to eternal life.

The woman who sought counseling concerning her marriage tells about the day her pastor taught on having a *relationship* with God – not just a religious belief. The pain and sorrow she was experiencing had made her heart tender toward the Lord; she realized that she had never been "born again." She had been trying in her own strength to fix things, but had never committed her life, heart, soul and spirit to a relationship with the living God.

The *relationship* she now has with the Lord has sustained her and given her hope for her marriage.

Jesus says, in the book of Revelation, "Behold I stand at the door and knock." He desires that we open the door to our hearts and allow Him to come *in*, transforming us into a "new creature" in Christ (2 Corinthians 5:17).

Now He can begin to change us. He gives us a chance to start over, to be renewed by His Spirit, to literally be born again. Once you are filled with His Spirit, the process doesn't end there. He continues to "do over" our lives, until we reach our final destination in heaven. "But we all . . . are being transformed . . . from glory to glory, by the Spirit of the Lord" (2 Corinthians 3:18).

We can also go back to Paul's letter to the Philippians in which God promises us, "He who has begun a good work in you will complete it until the day of Jesus Christ" (Philippians 1:6). When God begins the "do over," He starts a process that doesn't end until the day we leave this world and enter into the next. When Paul exhorts later in his letter, "Let this mind be in you which was also in Christ Jesus . . ." he is acknowledging the power of the Holy Spirit to change our minds, change our thinking, change our attitudes. All this can only happen after step one: being born again.

It is easy to feel religious at certain times of the year. The traditions of Easter, Christmas or the promise of a New Year tug at our hearts and fill us with spiritual longings. Weddings, funerals, births and other milestone events in our lives also cause us to think about our spiritual lives.

The challenge God puts before us – the opportunity – is to live every day of our lives in the presence of God. We don't need to save our religious experiences for a special occasion. Being a Christian means having a relationship with God, which is more than a religious experience. Like Nicodemus, we all need to have a face to face, mind to mind, heart to heart encounter with Jesus, the Son of the Living God – an encounter that carries us through every day of our lives and into eternity.

A FIRST STEP . . .

Just as a baby is first conceived, then grows inside its mother's womb before being born, the concept of a relationship with God often begins with a tiny seed of thought, or recognition of need in our lives. Just as Nicodemus knew that something was not quite complete in his spiritual life, even though he was very religious, I believe we all come to a point in our lives when a hunger gnaws at us and we need something more. We long to know what life is really about.

Jesus taught, "It is the Spirit who gives life; the flesh profits nothing. The words that I speak to you are spirit, and they are life" (John 6:63).

He also said, "He who hears my word and believes . . . shall not come into judgment, but has passed from death into life" (John 5:24).

Being born again is the result of you believing what Jesus taught, and receiving Him into your life. The Bible says, "But as many as received Him, to them He gave the right to become children of God . . ." (John 1:12). You can receive Jesus into your life simply by asking. Ask Him to forgive you of your sins, to come into your life, and to fill you with His Spirit. Then trust Him. Read His Word daily, and you'll discover what Nicodemus learned: what it means to enter into the Kingdom of God.

Now the attitude adjustments can begin!

CHAPTER TWO

THOUGHTS

The Battle Begins In Your Mind

Walking down a barren, parched, desert road in Israel, a Jewish man was attacked by a gang. The thugs stripped off his clothes, robbed him of valuables, beat him half to death, and left him to die

The road connected two cities, so it was reasonably well traveled. Along came a priest. He was probably busy with important things, so he took one look, moved over to the other side of the road, and walked on. Soon a Levite, or Temple assistant, came upon the wounded man, but after a moment's consideration, he too walked on.

Then a Samaritan man, a despised enemy of the Jews, stopped, assessed the injuries of the poor man lying

11

in the dust, and was moved with compassion. He tended his wounds, put him on his donkey, took him to a local inn, and paid for the man's care.

Jesus told this story to demonstrate the difference between *knowing* what is right and *doing* what is right; knowing the laws of God, as certainly the priest and Levite must have, and actually living them.

Did each of these men wrestle in their minds, even for a moment, about what they should do? Certainly, the Samaritan must have paused a moment before touching this Jewish man, knowing how much the Jewish people and Samaritans disliked each other.

His decision to be a "Good Samaritan" began with a wrestling match in his mind. Should I or shouldn't I? What's the right thing to do?

Many of the decisions and thought processes we engage in involve important, often life-changing choices. Our minds are the crucial battleground where matters of importance and eternal significance are being weighed and fought over every day. How we resolve these conflicts will make a profound impact on our lives and the lives of those we love.

THE BATTLE BEGINS IN THE MIND

There is a passage in my Bible that I've highlighted with a yellow marker. I also have certain parts of it underlined; certain words boxed; then the whole thing double underlined and the margin starred. It is truly one of the most significant portions of Scripture for me in my daily walk with the Lord and I believe it is the key to the abundant life Jesus promised us.

> "For though we walk in the flesh, we do not war against the flesh. For the weapons of our warfare are not carnal but mighty in God for pulling down strongholds, casting down arguments and every high thing that exalts itself against the knowledge of God, bringing every thought into captivity to the obedience of Christ."
>
> 2 Corinthians 10:3-5

As we live these words, experience them and incorporate them into our lives, I believe we conquer the fears, anxieties and problems that rob us of our joy. As we submit all of our thoughts to the Lordship of God, who loves us, the battle for our minds is won.

You see, it's just as the Scripture says. Flesh and blood and material things aren't what truly destroy us. The battle is for the mind. The devil's doorway to our soul is through the mind!

Even Charles Darwin once said, "The highest possible stage in moral culture is when we recognize that we ought to control our thoughts."

From a more spiritual perspective, the Danish theologian Soren Kierkegaard said, "Thoughts invite us, more than words and deeds, to continue in sin, for thoughts can be concealed, while words and deeds cannot."

The thought precedes the action. Look at the first sin in the Garden of Eden. How did Satan win that battle?

Did he wrestle Eve to the ground and force her to eat the forbidden fruit? No. He approached her mentally. He spoke to her thoughts. He enticed her into thinking in ways that challenged the Word of God. All he had to do was plant a little seed.

"Has God indeed said," the crafty serpent whispered into her mind, 'You shall not eat of every tree of the garden'? . . . You will not surely die. For God knows that in the day you eat of it your eyes will be opened, and you will be like God." (Genesis 3:1,5).

He worked on her mind! He dangled temptation in front of her. He played with her imagination, planting thoughts and ideas for her to entertain and share with Adam. Long before Adam and Eve's actions brought sin into the world, the battle was lost in their minds.

A DEVICE OF THE MIND

According to Vine's Expository Dictionary of the Bible, when the mind is being referred to in the New Testament, it speaks of feeling (emotions), judging (our thinking process) and determining (our will).

Vine's also notes that on at least three occasions when the original Greek word in the text is *psuche* (psyche, usually translated "soul"), it is translated into "mind." This is where we get our English word, psychology.

While there are six Greek words that are translated into "thoughts" throughout the New Testament, one Greek word, *noema*, is translated into both "thought" and "mind" in two key passages: 2 Corinthians 10:5 ("*. . . bringing every thought into captivity into the obedience of Christ . . .*") and Philippians 4:7 ("*. . . the peace of God, which surpasses all understanding, will guard your hearts and minds.*").

Noema means "a purpose or device of the mind."

How we think and how we allow our thought life to affect us becomes a tool or device with which we can do one of two things. We can submit our thoughts to the Lordship of Almighty God who wants to bless us and give us peace, love, joy and all the fruits of the Holy Spirit (Galatians 5). Or, we can allow the enemy to use this tool, this device of our minds, to gain the deadliest foothold of all into our lives – a chance to control and distract us through fear, anxiety, confusion and unbelief.

A distracted and confused Christian is not only miserable, but rendered virtually ineffectual for the Kingdom of God. Nothing pleases Satan more.

ONE THOUGHT, ONE MIRACLE
Naaman was a powerful man, the commander of the king's army in Syria. His story is told in the Old Testament in

the book of 2 Kings, chapter five. Right away we are told that he was honorable, respected, powerful and looked upon as a man "of valor." *But he was a leper.*

Leprosy was a dreaded, highly contagious and incurable disease that turned a person into a social outcast and eventually resulted in disfigurement and death. It is often used as an allegory for sin in the OId Testament. So the phrase, *but he was a leper*, completely undermines Naaman's list of achievements and accolades.

Naaman's wife had a young servant, an Israelite girl . The girl told her mistress about a prophet from Samaria who could heal Naaman of his leprosy. Eventually, through a letter to the king of Israel, Naaman was invited to visit this renowned prophet, Elisha.

And what did Elisha do with this man of great importance? He sent his servant out to him with a simple message: "Go and wash in the Jordan [river] seven times and your flesh shall be restored to you and you shall be clean."

Naaman was furious. Not only did this so-called prophet not even bother to come out and greet him personally, but he gave him these ridiculous instructions. Naaman went away complaining to himself, and anyone who would listen, *I thought he would at least come out and greet me. I thought he would call on the name of the Lord and wave his hand over me and heal my leprosy.* I thought. I thought.

Naaman was trapped in a mental wrestling match. He questioned the instructions, afraid of looking foolish. His pride was wounded. *After all,* he thought, *why the muddy Jordan River? The whole thing didn't make sense. Aren't there better rivers I could wash in and be clean?* "He turned and went away in a rage," the Scripture says. He came perilously close to missing the blessing God had for him, because his mind was stuck on, "I thought . . . ."

Finally, one of his servants came to him and tried to reason. "Hey, what have you got to lose? If the prophet had asked you to do something great, would you not have done it? Why not try this one simple thing?"

So Naaman, a desperate man, finally gave in. But I can imagine the mental turmoil churning through him with each dip in the water. An intense spiritual battle was being waged in his mind. He fought humiliation and no doubt the urge to get up and forget this foolishness. Finally, when he was done, after the seventh plunge, he came up and "his flesh was restored like the flesh of a little child, and he was clean."

What was his first public declaration? "Now I know that there is no God in all the earth except in Israel." (2 Kings 5:15). Oh how angry Satan must have been!

Naaman was healed, and more importantly, he came to know the One True God.

Just think how close he had come to allowing one thought to bar him from a miracle. One thought almost shut the gates of healing. One thought almost kept him from the goodness God. Yet, *one thought* of obedience led to the release of God's miraculous power in his life.

HIGHER THOUGHTS

Naaman needed an attitude adjustment. His pride was in the way. His thoughts were rebellious and angry. He was probably feeling sorry for himself. He was frustrated. All his worldly power and success couldn't do anything about the disease that was eating away his life.

We are all like Naaman in many ways. Our fears, anxieties and sinful thoughts are eating us up and threatening our lives and health as seriously as if we were afflicted with a deadly disease. Like Naaman, we too wrestle with humbling ourselves before God and doing the simple things He asks of us. Trusting Him. Willing our thoughts to be in agreement with His thoughts.

Simple? you say. It may sound that way, you argue, but it's not simple, and not easy. Our thoughts can overpower us before we even realize the war is on. So how do we bring our thoughts into obedience? How is it done?

Sometimes, like Naaman, we need to accept the counsel of godly people to point us in the right direction. And the right direction *always* takes us to the most powerful weapon we have – the Sword of the Spirit, the Word of God.

"Seek the Lord while He may be found," the prophet Isaiah encourages us. "Call upon Him while He is near. Let the wicked forsake his way, and the unrighteous man *his thoughts*; let him return to the Lord and He will have mercy on him." (Isaiah 55:6,7).

Later in the same chapter the Lord reminds us, "My thoughts are not your thoughts, nor are your ways My ways. For as the heavens are higher than the earth, so are My ways higher than your ways, and My thoughts higher than your thoughts."

God's thoughts are in His Word. We discover what the thoughts of God are by *daily* reading and meditating upon His Word and asking Him *daily* to help us focus our thought life upon Him. It is a battle, make no mistake. But it is a battle which God wants us to win.

It's been said many times that half the battle is recognizing your enemy. Now you know. Your enemy is not flesh and blood, not the things of this world, but every thought, imagination and every "high thing" that wants to loom higher, loftier and greater than the knowledge of God in your life. Remember, and try to grasp the fact that God says in His Word, **"My thoughts are higher than your thoughts."**

In the passage we will go back to again and again throughout this book, Philippians 4, we read, "Be anxious for nothing." Note: Did the apostle write, "Be anxious for . . . the important things? . . . a few things?"

No! He said, "for **NOTHING!** . . . and the peace of God, which passes all understanding, will guard your hearts and minds" (Philippians 4:7).

As we learn to think on the thoughts of God, found in His Word, then we can be assured, the battle has already been won.

> "Do not conform any longer to the patterns of this world, but be transformed by the renewing of your mind. Then you will be able to test and approve what God's will is — His good, pleasing and perfect will."
>
> **Romans 12:2 (NIV)**

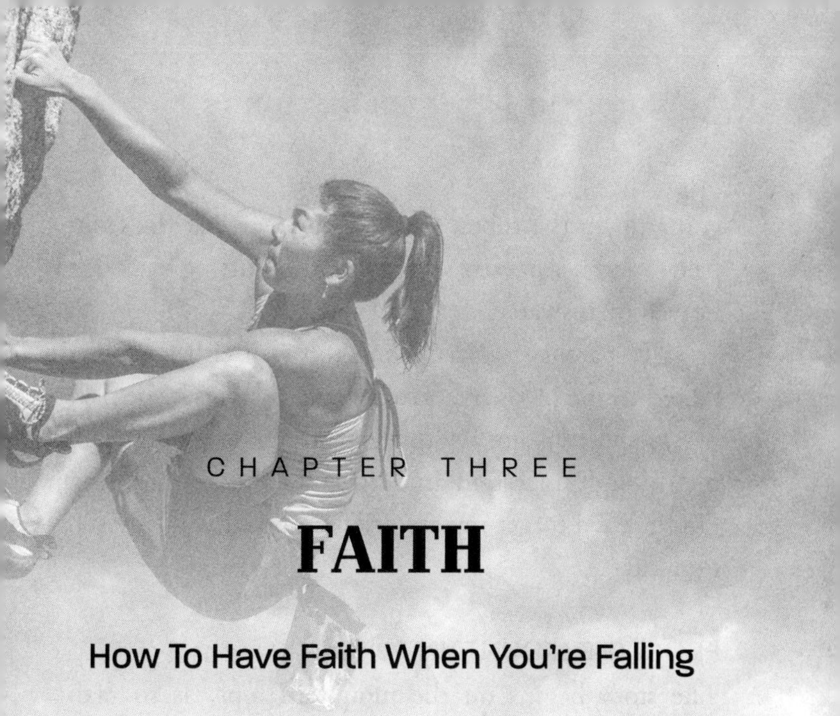

CHAPTER THREE

FAITH

How To Have Faith When You're Falling

God begins a good work in us, the apostle Paul wrote, which He promises to continue until "the day of Christ Jesus" (Philippians 1:6). In other words, during all of our earthly lives God will continue to work on our character and our attitudes.

I remember when two heartbroken parents came to me about their college age daughter. The young woman had called her parents, crying that she didn't think she could handle anymore. She had been through a devastating series of events, and in her eighteen-year-old world, everything was falling apart. Her heart was broken, her health was suffering, her college career was going down the tubes, she had no idea what the future held – and her prayers seemed to be bouncing back from heaven unanswered.

Her parents weren't doing too well either. As they talked to me of their heartache and feelings of helplessness, I shared a story with them which has often helped me through uncertain and difficult times – times when God needed to get my attention and deal with my state of mind.

FROM THE MOUNTAIN TOPS

The story begins on the mountain tops, as so many of God's lessons do. From the giving of the Ten Commandments on Mt. Sinai, to the Sermon on the Mount, to the return of Jesus on the Mount of Olives, mountains have often represented special revelations from God. This story is no exception.

Moses had just led the children of Israel out of Egypt. Three months into their journey, they stopped in the Wilderness of Sinai. After setting up camp, Moses went away to be alone and climb the nearby mountain.

As he reached the top of the mountain, Moses heard the Lord calling out to him, "Tell the people of Israel . . . what I did in Egypt, and how I carried you on eagles' wings and brought you to myself" (Exodus 19:3,4).

Years later, shortly before his death, Moses spoke to the entire nation of Israel, fulfilling the Lord's commandment.

"Ask your father," he urged the people. "He will tell you [about the time] when the Most High found him in a desert land, and in a wilderness, a howling wasteland. He shielded him and cared for him as the apple of His eye, like an eagle that stirs up its nest and hovers over its young, that spreads out its wings to catch them and carry them" (Deuteronomy 32:10-11, NIV).

EAGLES' WINGS

Moses used eagles as an analogy because he was familiar with their behavior, and he knew it was something his people would understand.

A mother eagle builds her nest on top of a mountain, usually on an unreachable crag jutting out of a cliff that oversees a chasm, thousands of feet below.

After the eagle builds a sturdy, safe nest, with all the twigs and material woven together, she feathers it. She cushions it for her babies with grass, feathers and whatever material will make it comfortable and cozy. When her eaglets are hatched, she spends the first weeks of their lives feeding them, sheltering them, seeing to it that they are nestled down in a warm and comfortable environment.

In this happy setting, they grow fat and strong. Soon they're wrestling around in the nest, elbowing each other for room, fighting to be first at the food line. Mom is wise. She knows it is time to disturb the nest.

Little by little she starts pulling out the feathers, the grass, the soft and cushy things. The little eaglets must be wondering by now, "What's with Mom?" as their nest begins to prickle and poke them. It's not so comfortable here. So they start working their way up from the bottom of the nest, trying to get away from Mom's antics, until they find themselves near the edge.

Wow! What a big world out there! They peek over the edge a bit, looking out at the horizon. It looks interesting, so they venture a little higher until they're perched right on the edge. Suddenly, Mom comes up from behind, thrusts out her big strong beak and pushes one little eaglet over the edge.

Well, at this point, our little hero is surely convinced Mom's crazy. He's falling and falling, apparently plunging to certain death, fighting the currents in the wind, vainly flapping his baby wings, tumbling around out there in the middle of the air, and no doubt scared to death.

Then, right before he hits bottom, Mom swoops down with her big powerful wings and catches him, carrying him up, up, up back to the nest, depositing him safely – until the next time.

Over and over, the eaglet tries to escape the new thorniness and prickliness of his nest. As he climbs to the perch, once again Mom pushes him out, and again he falls. Each time, Mom catches him, but she knows that one day soon she won't need to. Each time he falls, his flapping at the wind gets stronger and more sure. Finally the day comes when he is capable of flying on his own, soaring on the wind and learning to navigate all by himself.

And do you know how eagles navigate? By the sun. They look to the light for their guidance, as they fly off on their own.

RIGHT WHERE GOD WANTS YOU

The parallel to our children was certainly not lost on my friends as they watched their teenage daughter struggle to mature. Some of the hardships she endured were the direct result of her own choices. Some were simply life happening to a young woman whose time had come to leave the nest.

Her parents found that their nest was being a bit ruffled as well. They realized that not only did their daughter have lessons to learn about flying on her own, but they too needed to trust in God's promises. They had to lean solely upon the Lord, trusting Him to care for their precious child.

You see, God has perfectly placed the example of the eagles in nature to demonstrate how He deals with all of us.

C.S. Lewis once said, "What I like about experience is that it is such an honest thing. You may take any number of wrong turnings; but keep your eyes open and you will not be allowed to go very far before warning signs appear . . . the universe rings true wherever you fairly test it."

There are certain truths built into the universe, Lewis is saying. When we violate those truths, the consequences are warning signs. Signs that say "Danger!" or "Wrong Way!" Experience will teach us that certain things are good for us and some things are not. Experience teaches us that God's Word is true. But unless we venture out of the comfortable nest – or are shoved out – we won't ever learn what God has for us in this great adventure called life.

Oh, how we hate to have our nests disturbed! But do you know what happens to the eaglets if they are allowed to stay in the nest? They get so fat that they can't leave, and eventually they die.

God knows when it is time for us to learn to fly. Sometimes it's scary. Often it's painful. We can get so comfortable that we settle into habits that are not conducive to spiritual or mental growth. So God stirs the nest.

Then the next thing we know, we're shoved out of that place of complacency and inaction – and we're falling! "I don't know how to fly!" we cry. "I don't know how to deal with this. I can't do it alone!"

Now we're right where God wants us. Now when we pray, it's not out of some religious obligation. It's because

God has become our life line. Prayer is a necessity for survival, like breathing or eating. Prayer pours out of our being with no pretension or apathy, accompanied by a fervent desire to be solidly in God's care and will. Remember what Paul wrote to the Philippians? "Be anxious for nothing, but in everything by prayer and supplication, with thanksgiving, let your requests be made known to God" (Philippians 4:6).

Every trial we experience, every situation that makes us feel as if we're falling to certain destruction, is intended to bring us to a place of total faith in God and God alone.

GOD PREPARES THE WAY

It is important to remember, when we go through these learning experiences, that we are never alone.

Remember what Moses told his people? He reminded them that even as they were being shoved out of their nest, God hovered over them, like a mother eagle. He watched over them, "as the apple of His eye."

On another occasion when His people faced a new and terrifying situation, God encouraged them, saying, "See, I am sending an angel ahead of you along the way, to bring you to the place I have prepared. Listen carefully . . . do all that I say, and I will be an enemy to your enemies and oppose those who oppose you . . . Little by little, I will drive them out, until you have increased enough to take possession of the land" (Exodus 23:22-30).

This is God's continuing promise to us as He guides us through the wilderness experiences of our lives. When He stirs up our lives, and wants to teach us to fly, He not only hovers over us as a mother eagle, but He sends a powerful angel ahead of us to prepare the way. All He asks is that we trust in Him and listen to Him. He has so much to teach us, if we will allow ourselves to learn, and wait on Him for the results.

Little by little, the Scripture says, He will drive out our enemies. The lessons of life are not learned overnight, or through one incident. Little by little, step by step, He nurtures and instructs us.

He teaches us to fly, guided by the light of His Son, soaring on the wind of His Holy Spirit, and always – **always** – He will be there to catch us when we fall.

Only when we learn to trust Him while we're falling, can our minds focus on the good things of the Lord.

Re-read the fourth chapter of Philippians. Notice that Paul follows our key verse, "think upon these things," with "the peace of God will be with you."

Peace in the midst of falling is an attitude worth learning.

CHAPTER FOUR

POWER

Power Begins With Meekness

Iadmire the beauty, strength and unbridled passion of a wild horse. I think there's something in all of us that wants to be a little like that. At least I hope so.

No one wants to live life with a weak, defeated, too-tame attitude. Then all the adventure is gone! The zest is gone! It's important that your spirit, along with your passion, your strength, and your desire to live and run the race are not broken. A spirit broken in the wrong way leaves you with no desire or longing to live an abundant life.

On the other hand, an unbridled horse is of little use. It can even be dangerous to those around it. So how do we keep the fire alive without crushing the spirit? How do we live with total abandon and joy without hurting those we love or being insensitive to others' fears and failures?

MEEKNESS, NOT WEAKNESS

The Greeks used an interesting word to describe the taming of a wild and dangerous horse: *meekness*. The objective was to break the horse's will, to capture that unbridled power and energy, but never to break its spirit.

This is the same word that Jesus used when He said a curious thing to His followers: "The meek shall inherit the earth."

This must have shocked many of Jesus' followers. Meekness was pretty contrary to what they were looking for in a Messiah. They sought to conquer the earth through military and political domination. They desired material wealth that they could attain through hard work, self-assurance and self-assertion. But He said, "The meek shall inherit the earth." They misunderstood what He meant by meekness.

Picture a majestic, black stallion, caught out on the range and corralled. As it paws the ground and breathes its hot breath through flared nostrils, you can tell how restless and anxious it is to escape. You can't get near it, but you love it. It is powerful and charged with energy and reminds you of the horses who bore the knights of the round table, the princes and princesses in fairy tales and the cowboy heroes of the wild west.

But a horse that has a will of its own is of no use to its master – and neither is one with a broken spirit. It takes great wisdom and skill to break a horse's will without destroying its spirit. A horse with no spirit has no desire, no stamina, no readiness to go into battle with its master. You want it to have every ounce of its strength and vigor, but you also want it to be able to be guided. The horse, left alone, may be dangerous. But a horse that has learned to obey its master, responding to every signal and nudge, is a treasure to be cared for and loved and allowed to run to its full potential.

So when Jesus calls us to be meek, He is not calling us to be weak. On the contrary! He too wants to break our wills – but Jesus *never* broke anyone's spirit. He is the one who revives and strengthens our spirits (John 6:63). He longs for us to be so in tune with His will, that a mere sign or word will sharpen our spiritual senses and turn us in the right direction to be used to our fullest potential.

No one has ever suffered from a broken will. When our will is contrary to the will of God, and we make the decision to rebel against Him, then we take ourselves down a destructive path that renders our lives empty, futile, even useless. That's when people end up depressed, feeling as if life has no meaning. That's when the spirit breaks down.

JESUS WAS DANGEROUS

Jesus was called "meek and gentle" in 1 Corinthians 10:1. I believe that this description has too often been incorrectly interpreted.

We have efficiently pared the claws of the lion of Judah, as someone has noted, and have certified Him as "meek and mild," turning Him into a fitting household pet for pale curates and pious old ladies.

Yes, Jesus was tender to the unfortunate, patient with honest seekers and humble before heaven. But He rebuked respectable clergymen by calling them hypocrites. He referred to King Herod as "that fox" and was looked upon as a "gluttonous man and winebibber" because He wasn't afraid to be seen with the "wrong" people. He insulted the indignant tradesmen and threw them and their belongings out of the Temple.

Some considered Jesus dangerous – and He was, in the purest sense of the word. Too dangerous to have around. So they nailed Him to a cross, thinking that would silence this "meek and mild" man.

Aslan, the lion hero of C.S. Lewis' *Chronicles of Narnia*, is described as dangerous. Aslan is an allegoric character representing Christ, and in one scene some of the characters are discussing him:

"Then he isn't safe?" said Lucy.

"Safe?" said Mrs. Beaver. "Who said anything about safe? 'Course he isn't safe. But he's good. He's the King, I tell you."

Jesus is never safe to those who are cruel hypocrites.

His followers as well, with their meek spirits, are threatening to a world that seeks to break men's spirits and defy the will of God. Those who lived under Communist rule in Russia for 70 years will tell you who the real threat to that system was. It was those who were willing to lay down their lives for one another and their faith, just as Jesus did. It was in the Christian church that the real strength lay. Not in military might, not in political clout or materialism, but in the strength of a meek and gentle spirit. In the end, it was men and women and boys and girls who were on their knees praying to the God of heaven, who brought down the Communist system and the Berlin wall. The meek are inheriting Russia and Eastern Europe. The meek are praying against terrorism. Jesus said eventually, the meek shall inherit the earth. Meekness is not weakness.

What power and purpose lie in meekness!

The Bible calls Moses the meekest of all men. Do you know what made Moses meek? He was teachable. In spite of his insecurities and shortcomings, Moses allowed himself to grow and to learn. He was chosen to be the leader of his people, yet he never let that stop him from learning and taking advice from godly counsel. Leonard Ravenhill, the author and prayer warrior, was asked by a group of tourists about a certain historic village in Europe. They wondered if any great men had been born there. "Nope," he replied. "Only babies."

We all start out the same way. Why do some go on to lead successful productive, satisfying lives, doing great things for God, while others don't? I think the key is that you can never stop growing and learning. We are a generation mesmerized and pacified by television and videos and artificial life forms. Too many are zoning out on life, tuning out God, resisting His desire to tame our destructive wills and nurture our spirits.

2 Peter 1:3 says that "His divine power has given to us all things that pertain to life and godliness through the knowledge of Him who called us . . . ." The more we grow in the knowledge of God, the more we gain what is important for life. I believe that our happiness in this life comes as a direct result of growing in our relationship with Christ. When our will is subject to His will, our spirits will soar under the wings of His love.

If you feel as if your spirit is broken, and your will is out of control, then I'd like to suggest three things:

1. Humble your spirit and begin to worship God. Seek Him with your whole heart, seeking to have a personal relationship with Him. Spend

personal time with Him in devotion to His Word and prayer. Seek His will and ask Him to break you and fill you with His Spirit.

2. Educate your mind. I don't care how many degrees you have or what you've graduated from. Life is a long process of learning and growing. If you stop learning, you become BORING! If you have ceased to be curious and to ask questions, then you need to start again, like a child. Jesus said of children, "of such is the kingdom of heaven." Don't be satisfied with where you are now with the Lord. Feed on His Word, educate your mind and your soul. Grow.

3. Dedicate your body to active service. Romans 12:1 says, "Present your bodies a living sacrifice, holy, acceptable to God, which is your reasonable service."

A doctor from Seattle recently left a successful practice with a six-figure salary to help deliver babies in a run-down maternity ward in Moscow. She is using her own money to improve the ward and run it. Though she is rapidly depleting her savings and risking her financial security, she says she has never been happier in her life.

Stories abound of people who want to know that their lives are making a difference in this world. They are finding happiness in service, by working through churches, relief agencies, scouts, Sunday schools, home fellowships. Wherever God puts you, He will bless you for giving of yourself.

We are all looking for a mission in life, and I believe that God has the greatest mission of all. He has commanded us to love Him, to love our neighbors, and to go into the world to preach the Gospel, sharing His love.

Let meekness rule in your heart. It is a gift of the Spirit (see Galatians 5). It is what will make you ready to fulfill your heart's desire in the service of your Lord.

CHAPTER FIVE

VISION

Finding Meaning For Your Life

Helen Keller was once asked what would be worse than being born blind. She quickly replied, "To have sight and no vision."

She was a wise woman. Though she was physically handicapped by being born both blind and deaf, she had discovered one of the secrets to a successful life.

There have been others who knew the importance of vision – then lost it. When Alexander the Great had a vision, he conquered nations; when he lost it, he couldn't conquer a liquor bottle.

When David had a vision, he conquered Goliath; when he lost his vision, he couldn't conquer his own lust.

When Samson had a vision, he was known as a strong man who could easily defeat his enemies and serve as a judge for his nation; when he lost his vision, he didn't have the strength to resist Delilah.

When Solomon had a vision, he was the wisest man in the world; when he lost the dream, the vision God gave him, he couldn't control his passion for power and gold.

When King Saul had a vision, he was a mighty King; when he lost it, he was consumed by his own jealousy.

When Noah had a vision, he built an ark and saved the human race; when he turned from that heavenly calling, he got drunk and was humiliated.

When Elijah had a vision, he called down fire from heaven and was a mighty prophet on the mountain top for God; when he lost his vision, he ran from the wicked queen, Jezebel, and fell prey to fear and depression.

A vision, a purpose, and a calling on your life are important! "The glory of God is man fully alive," wrote Irenaeus, a second century theologian.

I would say that the apostle Paul was "fully alive." His passion for God motivated him to preach the Gospel at any cost; to risk his life and to pour himself into the lives of others. He wrestled with his own problems straight on. He cried out to God, "Oh, wretched man that I am! Who will deliver me?" He answered his own question by submitting himself, spirit, soul and body, to the Lord. He was never afraid to live for God, to love, to hurt, to plunge into this life to which God had called him.

But was he always that way? Somehow I doubt it. It was when Christ entered his life, first as an enemy, then as his Lord and Savior, that passion was kindled in Paul. He had been a student of the law, a Pharisee among Pharisees, he says by his own admission. I'm sure he had a zeal for the law and for being meticulously legal.

But that was nothing compared to what happened to him when Christianity exploded into his little world! First, he was threatened by this new Christian movement and became a relentless persecutor of the early church. Then he had a personal encounter with Jesus on the road to Damascus (Acts 9) that turned him around and made him Christ's greatest champion.

How was Paul transformed?

He tells us himself in Acts 26:12-19 when he was called to defend himself before King Agrippa. He related his encounter with Jesus and conversion, then summed up his discourse with these words: "Therefore, King Agrippa, I was not disobedient to the heavenly vision."

YOUR HEAVENLY VISION

Do you have a heavenly vision of your own? Do you doubt that God wants to give you one?

"Where there is no vision, the people perish," Proverbs 29:18 says. The Hebrew word translated into "vision" means a revelation from God. We need a vision from God to live! But I believe we have to be willing to listen to God and to submit our will to His. He takes us through a process, which I've outlined this way: Preparation, Participation, Purpose, Passion, and Power.

Preparation

The prophet Isaiah had an encounter with God, much like Paul, that completely changed his life. In Isaiah 6:1 he simply says, "I saw the Lord." then goes on to describe what he saw and what his response was: "Woe is me, for I am undone! Because I am a man of unclean lips."

Isaiah saw God in all His glory, then saw himself and his own sin. Next he describes an angel touching his lips with a live coal, pronouncing, "Your sin is purged." God put him through a purification process. He dealt with the sin in Isaiah's life, cleansing and preparing him for what came next:

Participation

Isaiah's vision of God changed him from a man who cried, "Woe is me," to a man who was ready to say, "Lord, here am I! Send me!" (Isaiah 6:8).

His vision had so radically changed Isaiah, that no longer would he be content to sit on the sidelines of life and watch the action. There would be no more wasted hours of idle entertainment, numbing his senses, bored, stunted and directionless. You see, not only had God touched Isaiah's life and dealt with his sin, He also gave him a purpose and a calling.

Purpose

Isaiah was called to be a prophet for God. There were dire needs in his time, an urgency to warn his nation of God's impending judgment. God's orders for him were, "Go, and tell this people . . . ." Then He told Isaiah what to tell them. God had a specific purpose for Isaiah's life, one that would give him a passion for living, a heart for others, and a mission for his life.

There is also an urgency in our times, to warn people that the Lord's return is drawing nearer and nearer.

But, you say, I'm not called to be a prophet! Maybe you aren't. Not everyone is supposed to be, according to Ephesians 4: "And He Himself gave some to be apostles, some prophets, some evangelists, some pastors and teachers, for the equipping of the saints for the work of the ministry, for the edifying of the body of Christ."

There is a place for each of us, a specific purpose and outlet for our gifts and talents. We need to be willing to commit ourselves to God's calling whole-heartedly, because I don't think He wants us to be lifeless, tired servants. He wants us to live with zeal and:

Passion

"Arise, shine; for your light has come! And the glory of the Lord is risen upon you!" Isaiah wrote much later (Isaiah 60:1).

What a difference in attitude! Isaiah is reveling in what God is doing in his life.

Jesus told us, "You shall love the Lord your God with all your heart, with all your soul, with all your mind . . . You shall love your neighbor as yourself" (Matthew 22:37-39). Paul exhorted his readers, "And whatever you do, do it heartily as to the Lord . . ." (Colossians 3:23).

These are not the words of half-hearted living. We are supposed to throw ourselves into life with a passion! We are to do whatever we do "heartily," not grudgingly, bored, and listlessly. That kind of living is a drag.

But I am bored, you cry! I hate my job, or school or life in general. I don't know how to live "heartily." None of us do, without God. "Without Me you can do nothing," Jesus said (John 15:5). Nothing that really matters, that is. That is why we need:

Power

"You shall receive power when the Holy Spirit has come upon you," we are promised in Acts 1:8.

"Most people lead lives of quiet desperation," Henry David Thoreau once wrote. That is the complete antithesis to the abundant life Jesus promises us.

Paul was obedient to the "heavenly vision." When we follow his example, I know that God will pour out His spirit upon us and give us a purpose, a passion and the power to live as never before.

Ask to be filled with the Holy Spirit every day of your life!

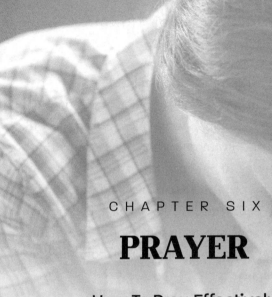

CHAPTER SIX

PRAYER

How To Pray Effectively

Be honest. What does prayer mean to you? A religious exercise? A duty? Something you want to do but you can't quite get with the program? Communion with God? A venting of feelings? An unburdening of trials? A cry in the dark? A one way conversation? A mystery? Maybe it's one of those things you're sure everyone else is better at than you.

"If we were perfected," C.S. Lewis once wrote, "prayer would not be a duty, it would be a delight."

We are not perfected, so we often struggle over the issue of prayer. But I would like to suggest that real prayer does not begin by gritting our teeth and "doing our duty."

Real prayer begins by falling in love.

By falling in love I don't mean that we pray only according to our feelings. Sometimes we don't feel like praying. It seems like another chore to get done. But by obediently coming to our heavenly Father with even our weakest most faithless prayers, He responds to our needs. As we begin to understand how much our heavenly Father loves us, our prayers become honest communication with Him. Religion turns into a relationship. Prayer becomes a delight.

BEGIN WITH WORSHIP

An effective prayer life is based on three foundations: Worship, Petition and Intercession. I believe that understanding these can help us tremendously in experiencing the kind of prayer that will change our lives and those around us.

Prayer is first of all, worship. People often ask me, how do I worship the Lord when I'm by myself trying to seek Him? We associate worship with singing in a congregation. But **worship begins by simply becoming aware that you are in the presence of God.** Open your spiritual eyes, and realize that when you cry out to God, "Father!" or "Lord!" or "Help!" you immediately enter into His presence.

The first form of prayer then is to realize you are not alone in this world. When Jesus came to earth in the form of man, the chasm between heaven and earth was bridged.

A wonderful way to begin praying is to turn to the Psalms and as you read, take into your heart and mind the praise, the worship, and the acknowledgment of who God is. In Psalm 19:1-2, David the psalmist was rejoicing over what he realized is the glory of God's creation: "The heavens declare the glory of God; and the firmament shows His handiwork. Day unto day utters speech, night unto night reveals knowledge."

Look at Psalm 25, another psalm of David. "To You, O Lord, I lift up my soul. O my God, I trust in You." By the time you finish this psalm, allowing these words to reach into your soul, you will indeed know you are in the presence of God. As you meditate daily on these Scriptures, prayer will pour out of you as naturally and easily as breathing.

"GIVE US THIS DAY . . ."

The second form of prayer should also come easily and naturally, because it is what we need to do so desperately as God's children: petition. Petitioning God simply means to bring our needs before Him and ask for His help.

Don't hesitate to cry out to God for wisdom. I go to Him often. I ask Him for direction when I'm confused. I ask for His provision when I am in need.

God wants His children to come to Him with their needs.

Amazingly, there are some people who call such personal prayers selfish. But Jesus Himself taught us to pray, "Give us this day our daily bread." He admonished His followers, "Ask, and it will be given to you; seek and you will find; knock and it will be opened to you. For everyone who asks receives . . . if you, being evil, know how to give good gifts to your children, how much more will your heavenly Father give the Holy Spirit to those who ask Him!" (Luke 11: 3; 9-13).

There is nothing wrong with going to God with our needs, daily. Don't wait for a crisis or "crunch" time. We need help *everyday*. Most of us have so many needs, that if we took them all to Him, we would be following the apostle Paul's injunction to "Pray without ceasing!" (1 Thessalonians 5:17).

Praying for our needs is what God desires from us. The greatest need we have is to be able to live in the center of His will, for only there will true life be. Only there will true peace lie.

It is not easy to stay on that "straight and narrow" Jesus described. Even Jesus, when He came to His Father with one of the greatest needs ever expressed, struggled over what He knew was God's will. In the Garden of Gethsemane He asked three times, "Take this cup from Me." He was in agony, Scripture says, so "He prayed more earnestly" (Luke 23-44). God's answer was not to change the course of events in this instance, but to strengthen Jesus to do what each of us needs the strength to do: surrender to our heavenly Father, echoing Jesus' words, "Not My will, but Yours, be done." That is the greatest need of all.

THE BATTLE

"Epaphras, who is one of you, a servant of Christ, greets you, always laboring fervently for you in prayer" (Colossians 4:12). That is how the apostle Paul described one of his co-workers, as one who labors in prayer.

Now that may seem to contradict what I've just said about prayer not being some sort of duty. This is different. This is intercession on behalf of others. This is when we reach out beyond ourselves and begin to pray for our family, friends, our church, for those with great needs. This becomes a true labor of love, as we realize that for those who are dear to us, the most important thing we can do for them is to pray.

The prayer of intercession is where prayer becomes a mighty weapon on the field of spiritual warfare. We are fighting for our loved ones, fighting for the will of God for their lives.

Paul describes the spiritual battle for us in Ephesians 6:11-18. Take the time to read that passage, where he describes the armor required of us.

We need to be armed with truth, the breastplate of righteousness, the gospel of peace, the shield of faith, the helmet of salvation and the sword of the Spirit. After Paul describes us being outfitted so magnificently, what does he say to do first? Stand there gleaming in the sun? No! Enter into the battle, **"praying always with all prayer and supplication . . . ."** The battle always begins with prayer.

You see, the earth rightfully belongs to Jesus Christ. He created it. He gave it to man, and man forfeited it to Satan. Jesus essentially went to Calvary to purchase back His creation, to prove that He loved us enough to die for us.

Jesus came to destroy "him who had the power of death, that is, the devil" (Hebrews 2:14). But Satan is not giving in easily. He wants to maintain control and will do it by force. He will fight as long as he can.

But Jesus also has a battle plan. He draws men and women into His kingdom through love.

When we enter into the battle praying for another individual, then we have truly entered a battle with the most powerful weapon of all. God has made prayer available to the weakest and newest of His children knowing that Satan must yield every time we pray in the name of Jesus.

Satan knows he is defeated each time you close your eyes to this world and open them to the other. He will try hard to discourage you because he knows that prayer will take you into a realm where the real battles of life are being waged, where what is truly important is being defended. He knows that prayer will enable us and empower us to live in God's will. As Chuck Smith said, **"I can do more than pray after I pray, but I really can't do more than pray until I have prayed."**

My prayer for you is that now, in your life, prayer will be a priority, not because you have made a resolution and you are going to grit your teeth and keep at it or else! But because you realize that prayer is what will draw you daily into God's presence, to be filled with His Spirit, encouraged and empowered to live a victorious life in Christ.

Pray without ceasing, for this truly is the will of God.

CHAPTER SEVEN

PROMISES

Hope For The Future

If you are about to leave on a journey and you know you aren't coming back, what would you leave behind for those you love?

Money? That would be nice. But what if your loved ones have needs that money can't take care of?

A beloved wife will need money to take care of her physical needs, but money will never replace the love relationship, nor fill her empty nights or ease the heartache she feels from losing a husband.

You know there will be heartaches, obstacles and hardships ahead for those you love. You know, because no one goes through this life without encountering such things.

Peter, the apostle, found himself in just this situation. He was writing one of his letters to his beloved church. He knew his own death was imminent. This particular letter, recorded in 2 Peter, is filled with warmth and love and encouragement. He wrote out of his own experiences of imprisonment and suffering to encourage other Christians facing the same trials and hardships. He wanted to leave behind for his brothers and sisters a treasure of immeasurable value. He wanted to tell them that no matter how hard it gets, there is hope!

The gift he left for them was the treasury of God's great and precious and absolutely infallible promises. These promises, which Peter recorded in the first century, are as relevant and valuable today as they were then. The Christians he specifically addressed were physically imprisoned for their faith. Having been there himself, he knew what they were enduring. But I think Peter also knew that prison walls are not always made of steel and stone. Circumstances have a way of trapping and enslaving us until we also feel like we're in prison. Maybe you aren't actually in jail – maybe you are – but certain elements of your life have imprisoned you.

Is it a job you hate? An unhappy and destructive relationship? Financial difficulties that make you believe you're trapped with no way out?

Physical impairments, like a devastating illness or a crippling injury can make our own bodies seem like a prison. Advancing age, wearing you down and slowing you down can make your life seem less productive. Any of these circumstances can make your life feel like a prison.

When you're convinced that you're trapped, it's easy to become depressed. You are nagged by thoughts of uselessness. Or you resent expending energy on something you hate, and feel like you're caught in a maze of meaningless work. Maybe you can't do much physically, and you feel unneeded and unproductive as life's minutes slip by with no real purpose or direction. It's especially hard if you remember a time when you were active, busy and what you did made a difference. Despair and despondency weave themselves slyly into the fabric of your life, making the prison even darker than before.

No wonder Thoreau the philosopher once wrote, "The mass of men lead lives of quiet desperation."

When we are immobilized, we tend to dwell on the past and wonder what went wrong. What did I do to end up like this? Past failures rise up to haunt us, like the ghosts of Scrooge's past in Dicken's "Christmas Carol," adding yet another reinforcement to the walls of our prison.

It's hard to have a godly attitude when you're in prison.

FREEDOM!

Peter understood this! He had done his time in jail, more than once. Being the kind of personality he was, I'm sure his attitude suffered tremendously during some of his prison stays. After all, this is Peter, the impetuous, hard driven, courageous apostle; quick to cut off a soldier's ear; quick to declare his love and loyalty to his Lord; ready to die for His master.

But Peter was slowed down more than once by prison, left to reflect upon his failures and to struggle with his attitude. And who understood what it means to fail more than Peter? After all, he denied Christ three times on the night of His suffering. I'm sure Peter never forgot.

But years later, close to his death, an older and wiser Peter sat down to pen words of encouragement to his fellow believers, because he knew, from the depths of his experience, that when the walls of life are closing in, there is freedom and hope in the promises of God.

"To those who have obtained like precious faith . . . grace and peace be multiplied to you in the knowledge of God and of Jesus our Lord," he wrote in 2 Peter 1:1-2. You can sense the enthusiasm in his heart when he writes of "precious faith" and "grace and peace" being multiplied in our lives!

Grace and peace be multiplied. When your life is a prison, what will conquer the despair that nags you? Peace! And how do you find it? Through the knowledge of God, Peter says. This is possible because, "His divine power has given to us all things that pertain to life and godliness through the knowledge of Him who called us . . ." (2 Peter 1:3).

"All things that pertain to life and godliness" is a pretty sweeping statement. But Peter understood what it meant to have a "knowledge of God."

Remember, Peter walked with Jesus. He talked to Him in the flesh. He ministered with Him.

But did Peter really know Him? It's been said that the longest distance between two points in the universe is the 18 inches between the head and the heart. We can have a head knowledge of God, memorize Scriptures and go to church. But how do those experiences and ideas work themselves into the core of our souls, into our hearts, causing us to truly know God?

It is one thing to walk with Jesus in the good times, like Peter did, following the Lord around the countryside, witnessing miracles and sharing the Good News. That is a glorious experience! But it is quite another experience to walk with Him through the valley of the shadow of death, to face suffering the way Christ suffered on the cross. The Christian life encompasses both.

When sin entered the world, death and corruption followed, afflicting the human race. God provided a way for us to be redeemed from our sin through His Son. He also provided a way for us to endure the suffering, to thrive in the prisons, and to escape "the corruption that is in the world" (2 Peter 1:4).

PRECIOUS FAITH, PRECIOUS PROMISES

Peter had discovered how "precious" faith is (verse one). Precious? A rough, hard-edged fisherman like Peter using the word precious? It makes me smile to think of it. Precious is also how he described the promises of God a few lines down.

Peter was different in his later years from the young, impetuous Peter who fervently declared to Jesus, "I will lay down my life for Your sake" (John 13:37), not fully understanding the nature of that commitment. Now, a more mature Peter, who had indeed suffered for his Lord, could identify with his fellow saints.

He didn't just say, "Yeah, I understand. Life is hard and that's the way it is." No, he gave them hope. He encouraged them, even in the midst of persecution, to focus their thoughts on the "exceedingly great and precious promises" of God. When we do that, he taught, "through these you may be partakers of the divine nature, having escaped the corruption that is in the world" (2 Peter 1:4).

These "great and precious promises" are not just platitudes, nice sayings, or bumper sticker material. No! Peter taught that by meditating on these promises, burying them in your heart, praying over them and living through them, we can actually become partakers of God's divine nature.

Bible commentator Herbert Lockyer took the time to count the promises of God in the Bible. There are 7,487!

Peter had learned the value of God's promises. He knew that they are true, that they can be counted on, that they are like treasures in our lives. They are nothing less than "precious." And if we as believers are not taking these promises and applying them in our lives, then we are spiritually poor, when we could be oh so rich in God's economy!

The promises in God's Word apply to all of life's situations. Believing His promises will help us turn our hearts and minds toward the things God wants us to think about, which takes us back to the key verse for this book: Philippians 4:8.

I would like to leave you with a few of the promises of God that have been important to me, but I encourage you to study and explore the Bible for yourself to find more. These are not just helpful hints. They are the very words of life, that will break down the walls of your prisons, lift you out of despair and give you the hope, strength and courage to carry on, as Peter did, until the day he died in the service of his Lord. The legacy Peter chose to leave for those he loved was the hope he had found in the "precious promises" of God.

Exceedingly great and precious promises:

> You will keep him in perfect peace, whose mind
> is stayed on You, because he trusts in You.
>
> **Isaiah 26:3**

The work of righteousness will be peace, and the effect of righteousness, quietness and assurance forever.

Isaiah 32:17

When you pass through the water, I will be with you; and through the rivers, they shall not overflow you.
When you walk through the fire, you shall not be burned, nor shall the flame scorch you, for I am the LORD your God . . . .

Isaiah 43:2-3

For I am the Lord who heals you.

Exodus 15:26

I will never leave you nor forsake you.

Hebrews 13:5

My God shall supply all your need according to His riches in glory by Christ Jesus.

Philippians 4:19

CHAPTER EIGHT

PURITY

How God Restores Your Innocence

She was caught in the most humiliating and embarrassing of circumstances – not to mention dangerous. Her deed was actually punishable by death. She was frightened, ashamed, desperate. What she didn't know, was that she was part of a drama that was fueled by moral, political, and spiritual issues.

She was caught in the act of adultery during a time when sexual immorality brought swift retribution in the form of public stoning. In the case of this particular woman, there was even more involved. She was set up. Jesus of Nazareth was teaching in the temple early one morning. He was not popular among the religious leaders of His day. They were constantly looking for ways to trip Him up, to catch Him off guard, to test Him and discredit Him. So they brought Him the guilty woman, and challenged Him: "Teacher, this woman was caught in adultery, the very act. Now, Moses, in the law, commanded us that such should be stoned.

But what do you say?" (John 8).

Before we get to Jesus' reaction, I want to ask: where was the man? I mean, this woman didn't commit adultery alone. And technically, according to Jewish law, both were to be stoned (Leviticus 20:10, Deuteronomy 22:22). Why was she singled out?

The scribes and Pharisees who brought her to Jesus were using her to get to Him. They didn't really care about righteousness or godliness. They didn't care about her. They had political motives for their actions. And, as we shall see later, Jesus turned it around and exposed their hypocrisy.

SEX FOR LOVE

But what about this woman? What was she doing risking so much for a man? Was she hoping for love? Was she a prostitute? We don't really know.

It's been said that men give love to get sex. Women give sex to get love. If you think this is hopelessly old fashioned thinking – that women no longer succumb to that kind of pressure – then talk to any group of young women at a college dorm, or a singles group. It happens. The tragic results lead to abandonment, heartache, unwanted pregnancies, abortions . . . hardened, bitter attitudes . . . and a burden of guilt and shame that I don't believe any human being was intended to carry.

But that's the way sin works. It entraps you and entangles you. One sin leads to another. Illicit sex creates unwanted pregnancies. Abortion looks like the easy way out. The sin is compounded, the memories more bitter, the hurt deeper. That's the way sin works.

One of my greatest heartaches as a pastor has been to discover how commonly couples – Christian couples, active in church – are involved in sexual activity outside of marriage. It grieves me because I know through counseling about the problems and pain that result. I also know that it's hard to resist! Sex is everywhere we turn. It's easy to rationalize. Here are a few lines that I've been told are tossed around with frequency in the singles and party scenes (If someone throws one of these at you, run!):

> » If you really love me, then you'll do it.

> » Life is so uncertain. It would be a shame to die without experiencing the greatest thrill of all.

> » I want to marry you someday and we should find out if we are sexually compatible.

» I promise we won't go all the way unless you want to. *(I'm sorry, but this is just not the way we were made. Once the engine gets going, we're gone!)*

» If you're afraid of your reputation, this will be our little secret. *(That is, until you break up or he gets to the locker room, whichever comes first.)*

» It isn't sex that I'm after. I'm in love. If you get pregnant I'll marry you. *(Not an easy way to start a marriage, by the way.)*

» Let's just live together to see how we get along. *(The divorce rate for couples who lived together before marriage is actually higher than for those who waited.)*

The beautiful experience God intended sex to be for a man and woman is ruined when we indulge outside of His will. The Bible says that sin is pleasurable only for a season, then comes judgment – and guilt.

Guilt? No one is supposed to feel guilty anymore. But we do! We try to rationalize our actions, relegating guilt into categories like "negative thinking." We fight it, and we try to tell ourselves, and even our kids, as long as you play it safe, it's OK.

But it's not OK, because God calls it a sin. If you feel guilty, it could be because *you are*. Sin separates us from God, and eventually we are left with an emptiness in our souls which all the physical pleasure in the world can't fill. In fact, after awhile it's no longer satisfying. Guilt steps in, and our whole attitude toward love and sexuality becomes tainted by sin.

Sex is intended to bind a man and woman together in a unity of spirit, soul and body that can only be experienced through the commitment of a godly marriage. Only then, can sex be experienced at its best. It remains pleasurable, satisfying, and blessed by God.

Outside of marriage, sex becomes a desperate tug of war between two people who are often selfish, uncommitted, and struggling to find satisfaction where only emptiness of soul lies. There's nothing worse than to be sexually active and not enjoying it. That's not how God intended it.

I also don't need to remind you that sexual immorality carries some terrible physical consequences. The number of patients with AIDS and other sexually transmitted diseases has increased with each generation. Every time we engage in immoral sexual behavior, we gamble with our lives, and add another bullet to the chamber.

The apostle Paul wrote bluntly of immorality, "Those who practice such things will not enter the kingdom of heaven." Every time you fall to sexual sin, you gamble with your soul, your body and your spiritual life. It's simply not worth it.

BEEN THERE, DONE THAT

But I've already been there, you say. I can't undo it. I'm like the woman caught in adultery. Now what do I do?

First of all, let's look again at this woman's situation. The Pharisees were so smug. Here they had dragged her before Jesus, not caring about her. They just wanted to see what He would do. After all, on the one hand He had gone about the country preaching love and forgiveness and compassion and breaking tradition left and right. On the other hand, He claimed he had never broken the law of Moses. So what would He do with her?

Can you imagine this woman's humiliation? I picture her thrown down on the ground before Jesus, like some prize catch. As she sat in the dust, weeping for shame or bracing herself against what was to come, Jesus simply knelt down and wrote something in the sand with His finger. We don't know what He wrote, but what He said gives us a clue: "He who is without sin among you, let him throw a stone at her first" (John 8:7). Again he stooped down to write.

Was He writing the names of guilty ones? Lists of sins? One by one, the men withdrew, stricken in their consciences, until Jesus and the woman were left alone. He had demonstrated that those men had no right to judge her. But now she was face to face with the Lord. What would He do? Looking around, He asked her, "Woman, where are those accusers of yours? Has no one condemned you?"

Imagine her emotions, as she looked Jesus in the eye and began to grasp that she had just been saved from a horrible death. "No one, Lord." She acknowledged Him as Lord – something the Pharisees had certainly not done – as she saw in His eyes acceptance, love and compassion.

"Then neither do I condemn you," He said. What relief! "Go and sin no more."

PURITY AND LOVELINESS RESTORED

She had also been saved from a horrible life. He called her "woman," a term He had only used for His mother and for the other Mary on the morning of the resurrection. He gave her the dignity of her womanhood back, bestowing upon her the very name Eve was given. This implied a respect she had not received from men for a very long time, if ever. All these things, Jesus restored to her, while soundly putting the hypocritical Pharisees in their place.

Philippians 4:8 tells us to think upon "whatever things are pure, whatever things are lovely." I'm sure it had been a long time since this woman thought herself as pure or lovely. But now, through the eyes of Jesus Christ, through His saving grace, her purity and loveliness had been restored.

The next words Jesus spoke to those watching on the sidelines were, "I am the light of the world. He who follows Me shall not walk in darkness, but have the light of life."

Being caught in the act of our sins is like having a heavenly light suddenly turned on us. It can be embarrassing. Humiliating. Painful.

The woman above was caught, out in the open, in front of neighbors, friends, peers. Sometimes we aren't caught so blatantly, but it is a fact of life, that eventually our sins will find us out. There are consequences to our actions. When God tells us not to do certain things or behave in certain ways, it's not because He's out to ruin all our fun. It's because He knows what is good for us, what will lead to healthy, fruitful lives, and what will lead to destruction.

What would have happened to the woman "caught in the act" if her life had continued the way it was going? If she had never encountered Jesus? I don't think it's too hard to figure out that her life was not going anywhere good.

Have you had an encounter with Jesus? Are there aspects of your life that you know, deep down inside, will eventually hurt you or lead to nowhere good?

Read what the prophet Jeremiah wrote about a life yielded to the Lord:

"Blessed is the man who trusts in the Lord,
   And whose hope is the Lord.
For he shall be like a tree planted by the waters,
   Which spreads out its roots by the river,
and will not fear when the heat comes;
   but its leaf will be green,
And will not be anxious in the year of drought,
   Nor will it cease from yielding fruit."

Jeremiah 17:7-8

If, like the woman, we can acknowledge Jesus as Lord, and realize that He understands our human frailties and sees right through hypocrisy and judgmental accusers, then we too can step out of the darkness into the light, into a new life. We can be clean and pure once again.

"There is therefore now no condemnation for those who are in Christ Jesus" (Romans 8:1).

CHAPTER NINE

MARRIAGE

How Marriage Reflects
God's Attitude Toward us

When a young couple comes to me and says they want to get married and could I perform the ceremony, I'm honored. Weddings are one of the best parts of being a pastor. And in spite of our modern morality, marriage is still one of the major events in most peoples' lives. Sometimes that puzzles me.

The church ceremony is just one facet of what often becomes a complex and expensively orchestrated social event. Yet in spite of all the time, trouble and money that goes into a wedding, there is not always a clear understanding of what marriage is about.

God invented marriage. He instituted it. He put it together. He sustains the institution. He blesses it. The whole thing was His idea. I can't figure out why anyone who does not want to obey and trust God, would want to follow this ancient practice of a man and a woman committing themselves to one another, seeking to live together in fellowship and intimacy throughout their days.

Marriage is more than a binding legal formality. When two people stand before God, family and friends and pledge their vows, they are making a commitment not only to each other, but to God. Why bother, unless God matters?

GOD SAVES THE BEST FOR LAST

Looking at the very first marriage might provide some answers.

After God created the heavens and the earth, He created man (Genesis 1).

Adam was created, the Bible says, in the image and likeness of God. Adam was intelligent, noble, "Sprung from the soil yet descended from above. Fashioned of the dust yet inspired by celestial breath. Allied to the beasts, yet the offspring of God."[2] He lived in a virtual paradise. He was the overseer of all creation. He was richly endowed with immortality, intelligence, and best of all, he

---

2   Redford, R.A., *Pulpit Commentary, Vol. 1*, p. 53, MacDonald Press.

was in constant communion with God. His life should have been perfect!

But Adam was lonely. Obviously he was not created to be complete in himself. So, God created woman. Truly, He had saved the best for last!

The very first marriage ceremony, began with God pronouncing, "It is not good that man should be alone." It was completed by Adam's heartfelt declaration, "This is now bone of my bones and flesh of my flesh and she shall be called woman for she was taken out of man."

Eve became Adam's wife, his companion, his helpmeet, his soul mate. Together they found an intimacy and fellowship that could not be found through any other means.

After His last and best creation, the very first societal arrangement God placed on this earth was the institution of marriage. The only way to really understand the depth of the marriage commitment is to study God's intentions through the Scriptures.

COMPLETE COMPANIONSHIP

Look at the way God created Eve.

Genesis 2:21 says, "And the Lord God caused a deep sleep to fall on Adam, and he slept; and He took one of his ribs, and closed up the flesh in its place. Then the rib which the Lord God had taken from man He made into a woman and He brought her to the man."

There are two interesting points here. First, God put Adam to sleep. The Hebrew word for sleep, accurately translated, means a state more like anesthesia. It's as if God put Adam under anesthesia and performed surgery on him. Secondly, "rib" is a poor translation. The same Hebrew or Greek word is used 35 times in Scripture, and in at least 20 instances it is more accurately translated as "side." It was from Adam's side that the woman was created. As others have noted, she came neither from the man's head to rule over him, nor from his feet to be inferior to him, but from his side, nearest his heart, signifying total equality and complete companionship.

But why anesthesia? Pain and suffering would not enter the human equation until after the fall, so this "sleep" was not necessary. Interestingly, the analogy of "sleep" is the same analogy Jesus used to describe death for the believer. Adam "died" to receive his bride.

Do you see a picture here of Jesus Christ and His Church? While Jesus suffered on the cross, a Roman soldier took a spear and thrust it into His side; out of this wound gushed water and blood.

When Genesis says that God opened up Adam's side, from which He took flesh and blood and bone, the literal translation is that He "built" a woman. "On this rock I will build my Church," Jesus said. His Church, His Bride.

Ephesians chapter 5 teaches us that the Church has a heavenly Bridegroom who went into a deep sleep of death, in whose body not a bone was broken but whose flesh was torn at the side. From the life of Adam God created Eve. From the life of Christ He built the Church, the Bride of Christ.

Ephesians 5 goes on to describe God's plan for marriage, but begins with the exhortation to all believers to submit "to one another in the fear of God" (5:21).

Next, Scripture states, "Wives, submit to your own husbands." This does not, however, *ever* give a husband the right to dictatorially demand of his wife that she "submit!" We begin by submitting to one another.

Now look at verses 25-29. Husbands are to "love your wives, just as Christ loved the Church and gave Himself for it."

How did Jesus love the Church? He died! He was crucified! He was nailed to a cross, fulfilling His vow and commitment to His Bride, to us, even when we were unresponsive to His love; even when we rejected Him, turned against Him and broke our own vows and commitments. Still, Jesus loved us enough to die, knowing that not all would receive Him – that ultimately we would crucify Him.

Jesus didn't back away when things got hard. He never said, "Well, it just didn't work out." No, He gave everything to His Bride. The commitment He made was not contingent on His feelings or on circumstances. He fulfilled His promises, and we can thank God He did.

GREATER LOVE

This is the example given to every man who goes into marriage. When couples stand in a church and pledge before God and their family and friends, ". . . 'till death do us part," what do those vows mean? Obviously, in to-day's culture with the high divorce rate, they don't always mean much.

This is why I'm sometimes puzzled at the popularity of marriage. Why bother with a God-ordained institution if God is squeezed out of the picture? Perhaps it is because there is a place in everyone's heart that wants what Adam and Eve had – *intimacy, companionship, commitment.* But until we understand the true nature of marriage, according to God's will, people in and out of marriages will continue to be lonely and unfulfilled, just as Adam was.

Marriage is more than a legal contract, more than a system for social organization. The Bible says, "Greater love has no one than this, than to lay down one's life for his friends" (John 15:13).

If a man were to truly follow Christ's example and lay down His life, crucify his own selfish desires and want nothing more than his wife's happiness, oh how easily his wife would respond to him, how tenderly her heart would reciprocate. How willingly a wife would become a "helper" (Genesis 2:18). (I hope that women will never take "helper" as an inferior, demeaning position. The term is often used to describe God Almighty Himself; see Psalm 33:20, 70:5, 115:9.)

Yet daily, our society tramples upon the sanctity of marriage. And daily I see people who are lonely, much as Adam was; people who have seemingly successful lives, even marriages, but something is wrong, and emptiness and loneliness prevails.

One of the first things I do when I am asked to perform a marriage ceremony, is talk with the couple and find out where they stand spiritually.

Before they can fully commit their lives to each other, I believe they need to be fully committed to Jesus.

This may sound like tough terms, but it is only because I know that without the Lord as a starting point, this marriage's chance of survival is minimal. Few things are more heartbreaking than a love grown cold, or even worse, a love reduced to bitterness and hatred.

If you are married and struggling to hold it together, I encourage you to seek some Biblical counseling, to keep your commitment to each other, trusting that God has a wonderful plan for you. If you are getting married, take God's plan to heart, and hold it dear as the path to a truly fulfilling and lasting marriage.

I believe that God would want us to apply the principles of Philippians 4:8 toward our spouses. Think about what you know is true, noble, lovely, and virtuous about the one you love. Paul writes, "If there is anything praiseworthy, think upon these things." Rather than dwelling on the faults of your mate, look for what is praiseworthy, what made you fall in love, what you admire and respect about him or her. Doing this will change your attitude toward your marriage tremendously.

Remember the example of Jesus. Love is not getting but giving. It is not seeking for yourself, but giving all. It's laying down your lives for one another, putting each other's well-being and happiness above your own. Truly that is the key to a happy marriage, and the attitude God desires in us.

CHAPTER TEN

WORRY

Transforming Worries Into Peace

A friend said to me one day after I asked her how she was doing, "Oh, I'm fine today, but I'm sure tomorrow will take care of that."

My heart went out to her because I knew this was a woman beleaguered and burdened by worry and anxiety.

Worry is a disease that robs you of your vitality, your enthusiasm for living, and even your health. Medical doctors and psychologists agree that many ailments, aches and pains are caused by something much less tangible, the anxiety of the soul. Ralph Waldo Emerson once spoke of "the torments of pain you endured, from evils that never arrived."

Worry can become a lifestyle, a habit that shapes your attitude and erodes away your faith. The habit of worrying can gain such a stranglehold on your life that it becomes part of your personality. You find yourself approaching every new situation or event with an anxious attitude. Worry becomes a constant companion, a burden that weighs you down and slows you down. Worry can change your physical countenance. A heavy heart will rob you of your joy and your ability to see beyond the nagging complexities of daily life.

That sounds a bit exaggerated, you say. I mean, we all worry a little don't we? It's a normal human emotion! Yes, it may be normal. But let me take it a step further. It's not only a disease. It's a sin.

"Worry is an old man," I once read, "with a bended head, carrying a load of feathers which he thinks is lead." Worry is a sin because it violates some of the most basic commandments of God and because it robs us of a close relationship with Him. It causes us to carry burdens that our Heavenly Father never intended us to bear, and to turn what in reality are small matters, better left to God and His wisdom, into heavy, devastating circumstances.

PERFECT PEACE

"Be anxious for nothing," Paul wrote to the Philippian church. "But in everything by prayer and supplication, with thanksgiving, let your requests be made known to God; and the peace of God, which surpasses all understanding, will guard your hearts and minds through Christ Jesus" (Philippians 4:6-7).

This very human emotion is a process of our minds, of imaginations out of control, of being too focused on ourselves and our own inabilities to cope. Instead, Paul exhorts, we need to turn our thoughts to God, and go to Him with *all* our needs. He promises in return, to give us peace, and to guard our hearts and minds against those fears and anxieties that would destroy us. What a relief it is to give our worries to Him!

The apostle Peter entreats us, "Humble yourselves under the mighty hand of God, that He may exalt you in due time, casting all your cares upon Him, for He cares for you" (1 Peter 5:6-7). I like the French translation of that verse, which reads, "Unload your distress upon God." The Phillips Modern English translation puts it, "You can throw the whole weight of your anxieties upon Him."

It is interesting that Peter began that thought with "Humble yourselves." It is humbling to acknowledge that we cannot take care of everything ourselves. Worry becomes a sin when it takes over our thought processes and reflects a lack of faith in God's ability to work out the details of our lives. "Anxiety is not only a pain which we must ask God to assuage," C.S. Lewis said, "but also a weakness we must ask Him to pardon – for He's told us to take no care for the morrow."

Worry is a reproach to God; it grieves Him, because after all, didn't He promise "I will never leave you nor forsake you" (Hebrews 13:5)? If we believe that, then we are saying, "I know You're here. I just don't think You either care enough or are capable of helping me with this situation."

One day Peter and the other disciples were out on the open sea in Galilee when a great storm came up. Jesus, weary from days of ministering, had fallen asleep, only to be awakened by the worried and terrified cries of His friends, "Master! Master! We are perishing!"

Jesus immediately calmed the wind and the raging sea, then turned to His disciples and gently rebuked them. "Where is your faith?" He asked.

Where is our faith when we worry and fret and allow the complexities of life to gnaw away at our peace?

Again and again Peter saw Jesus calm the storms of people lives, settle the raging waters, heal their pain, fill the fishermen's nets with fish to overflowing, bring peace and happiness back into His followers' lives. Peter knew what he spoke of when he reminded us to "cast our cares upon Him."

THREE BURDENS

We carry three heavy burdens with us through life: the past, the present and the future.

The **past** is capable of producing a tremendous load of anxiety and worry in the form of regrets, guilt, unconfessed sin, unhappy memories, and neglected duties. Worry about the past will plague our present.

I know of a young woman who spent years worrying about whether her abusive past would prevent her from being a good wife and mother. Finally, she grew to believe what the Bible promises: "If anyone is in Christ, [she] is a new creature; old things have passed away; behold all things have become new" (2 Corinthians 5:17). There is freedom in those words! When we can fully grasp the fact that God can bring us new life, then we can also put away the fears of what haunts us and hurts us from the past.

Oswald Chambers writes, "Our yesterdays present irreparable things to us . . . but God can transform this destructive anxiety into constructive thoughtfulness for the future. Let the past sleep, but let it sleep in the bosom of Christ."

The **present**, however, never seems to sleep or allow us to rest when it is filled to overflowing with nagging doubts and worrisome details. The choices we have to make, the trials we endure, the obstacles toward meeting deadlines, finishing tasks, taking care of families, traffic jams, health worries, financial worries – all of it can give us headaches, ulcers and heartaches.

Remember Martha? She was the harried hostess in the book of Luke (chapter 10). She bustled around, fretting over preparations for a social event, not enjoying herself at all, until, exasperated, she cried to her guest, Jesus, "Lord! Don't you care?" Jesus answered her, "Martha, Martha, you are worried and troubled about many things. But one thing is needed . . . ."

The thing that was needed was for her to sit down at Jesus' feet, take in His presence, listen to His Word, and allow peace to be restored in her heart.

I'd like to quote Oswald Chambers again: "Are you looking unto Jesus now, in the immediate matter that is pressing, and receiving peace from Him? If so, He will be a gracious benediction of peace in and through you. But if you try to worry it out, you obliterate Him."

"Worry it out." That's what we do, thinking that we are somehow going to affect the outcome of events. That's how many of us approach our **futures**. The ancient philosopher Seneca said, "The mind that is anxious about the future is miserable."

And what a tortuous misery that is! When we worry about things that have not yet happened, we torture ourselves mentally and emotionally, allowing our whole attitude and countenance to be warped into nervous, fretful anxiety.

The Scriptures are full of so many wonderful exhortations and encouragements about the future, but nothing is more profound yet straightforward than Jesus' words from the Sermon on the Mount:

"Do not worry about your life, what you will eat or drink; nor about your body, what you will put on. Is life not more important than food and the body more important than clothing? Look at the birds of the air; they do not sow or reap or store away in barns, and yet your Heavenly Father feeds them. Are you not much more valuable than they?

"Who of you by worrying can add a single hour to his life?

"And why do you worry about clothes? See how the lilies of the field grow. They do not labor or spin. Yet I tell you that not even Solomon in all his splendor was dressed like one of these . . . So do not worry . . . But seek first the kingdom of God and His righteousness, and all of these things will be given to you as well.

"Do not worry about tomorrow, for tomorrow will worry about itself" (Matthew 6, NIV).

THE CURE FOR WORRY

So what's the cure for worry? One word: trust. Total trust in our Heavenly Father, in His love and caring provision for us in every aspect of our lives.

But we can't trust someone we don't know. So I encourage you to take the time daily to be in His Word and to seek Him in prayer.

This may sound like a worn-out Christian cliche, but it is honestly the simplest, most basic and absolutely reliable answer I know of for fighting off worry. We can choose to live our lives under the burden of worry, or we can choose to adopt an attitude of trust, through which God wants to bless us.

Remember, the Lord is your Heavenly Father, who loves you very much. He wants nothing more than to take your burdens, fears and anxieties and replace them with His peace, His love and the joy of living in His care.

CHAPTER ELEVEN

COMFORT

How To Handle The Pressures Of Life

Forrest Gump says, "Life is like a box of chocolates. You never know what you're going to get."

That may be true, but sometimes I feel more like a balloon. When things are going fine, I can cruise above the clouds, rise above my problems, and flow in the jet stream.

Until a crisis hits. One of the kids gets sick. There's a problem at work. A car breaks down. A death in the family. A new heartache. A new financial crisis. Now the pressure is on . . . and I feel more like a balloon that has popped under pressure. I'm flying around with the air running out, in no particular direction, doomed to finally fall to the ground, deflated and broken.

That is when most of us start looking at our lives and asking questions like, "Am I really happy?" And if not, "why not?" The "pursuit of happiness" which is, after all, a constitutional right, has become somewhat of an obsession in our society. We look for happiness as a means for escaping the pressures of life. Unfortunately, I believe we are asking the wrong question.

Rather than "Am I happy?" the relevant question is, "Am I faithful and obedient to the Lord?" C.S. Lewis once wrote, "God cannot give us happiness apart from Himself because it is not there. There is no such thing." The Bible promises us, "Blessed is the man who walks not in the counsel of the ungodly . . . but his delight is in the law of the Lord" (Psalm 1).

The "pursuit of happiness" too often leaves us discouraged, and even more unhappy. When things don't go our way, we get even more depressed and discouraged. Happiness is not the right starting place.

Discouragement is no respecter of persons. Even people of great faith, like Charles Spurgeon, go through such times of desperation that Spurgeon once wrote, "I am the subject of depressions of spirit so fearful that I hope none of you ever get to such extremes of wretchedness."

It was this kind of despair that drove the apostle Paul to write a letter to a young struggling church in Corinth, Greece.

The seaport of Corinth was a wealthy economic center with international trade. But the church was in trouble. Their lives were full of stress and temptation, and many of the believers had succumbed to the pressures of their surroundings. Backbiting, murmuring, complaining, despair and discouragement were threatening to overwhelm them. They were in desperate need of an attitude adjustment.

Paul deeply loved this church. His desire was to strengthen the people in their faith, as he wrote, **"Grace to you and peace from God our Father and the Lord Jesus Christ . . . the Father of mercies and God of all comfort who comforts us in our tribulation."** (2 Corinthians 1:1-11).

The Greek word used for tribulation here is literally translated as pressure. It's the sensation you would experience if someone pressed down on your head and tried to push you into the ground. You would feel the strain in your neck and your shoulders. The tension would permeate your whole body. Sound familiar?

Paul wrote from the heart of experience. He understood trouble. "We do not want you to be uninformed, brothers, about the hardships we suffered," he wrote. "We were under great pressure, far beyond our ability to endure, so that we despaired even of life. Indeed, in our hearts we felt the sentence of death" (2 Corinthians 1:8).

Paul knew that his fellow believers were dealing with more than skinned knees or a bad day at the office. He knew about life and death situations. He knew about losing loved ones, about painful relationships, about setbacks in his life's work. He knew about pressure. He knew what it meant to "despair even of life."

GOD PERMITS TRIALS

When he spoke of comfort, it wasn't in nice religious platitudes. The word he used for comfort comes from the Latin word *fortis*, meaning strength. He knew that his fellow believers would have to grow strong in their faith, if they were to survive the pressures they faced.

One of our first reactions when pressure bears down, is to become overwhelmed by our circumstances and to start asking, "Why?" It's as if we forget that God is there. We stop worshiping and praising Him and fail to realize that trials are a part of life for one of three reasons.

First, trials come simply because we are human beings living in a fallen world where things are not perfect. We cannot help but be affected by what goes on around us. Secondly, trials afflict our lives when we are disobedient. There are consequences to deliberately going against the will of God. Thirdly, the truth is, trials come because God permits them.

What? God allows these things into my life? Yes, and Paul explains why: **"In our hearts we felt the sentence**

of death. But this happened that we might not rely on ourselves but on God . . . On Him we have set our hope."

When the pressure comes bearing down and we cannot cope, God wants us to know that there is no place to turn but to Him. He wants us to realize our weakness, so that we will set our hope on Him and Him only.

A friend of mine has a unique way of ministering to people. She's about 70 years old and has been a part of our church since its beginning. She lives on a boat.

When you visit her, she'll motion for you to follow her to the end of her boat, and invite you to step down into the little dinghy tied to the stern. Then with a pleasant smile, she'll settle in and begin rowing. Your destination is somewhere out in the middle of the bay, where she'll often pull up the oars, and invite you to say what's on your mind.

My friend is a good listener, and has heard countless hours, no doubt, of people's problems and tribulations. She is sympathetic and concerned, but her advice is often simple and direct. She'll pat your hand or look at you and say, "You've got your eyes on yourself, instead of God."

She's usually right. It's not wrong to hurt. It's just that it hurts more when we focus on our circumstances rather than on what God wants to do.

Why should I praise God, you ask, when there is so much wrong in my life? Because . . . He is God. And because, if you believe in Him, then you are "beloved of God" (Romans 1:7). He is, Paul wrote, "the Father of mercies." When the Hebrews used the term "father of" they meant the originator, the author of. God is the originator of all mercy, and His mercy is "manifold" (Nehemiah 9:19) and "tender" (Psalm 25:6) and there are "multitudes" of His tender mercies for each of us (Psalm 51:1). *It is God's very nature to comfort you.*

THE COMFORTER

When Jesus was preparing to bodily leave this earth, He told His disciples that He would never leave them alone: "the Holy Spirit, whom the Father will send in My name, He will teach you all things, and bring to your remembrance all things that I said to you. Peace I leave with you" (John 14:26-27). In these verses, the Holy Spirit is titled, in various translations, Comforter, Counselor, Helper.

The world can throw at you what it will, Paul wrote, but it will not overwhelm you. "For just as the sufferings of Christ flow into our lives, so also through Christ our comfort overflows. If we are distressed, it is for your comfort and salvation; if we are comforted, it is for your comfort, which produces in you patient endurance" (2 Corinthians 1:5,6).

The attitude we maintain during times of suffering will determine our ability to endure. If we can adopt

Paul's attitude – that we should be anxious for nothing, that we can take everything to God in prayer, that He will give us peace and enable us to "do all things through Christ" – then we can endure anything! The Greek word Paul used for endure means more than just getting through. It connotes **overcoming in triumph**! Just as silver becomes purer and finer by going through intense heat, so the Christian can emerge stronger and finer through the trials we endure.

You can be pressured, perplexed, persecuted and hurt, but when your hope is set on the Lord, He will fill you with His Spirit, and give you the strength, help, and counsel to endure, to triumph and to live in the blessings of a merciful and loving God. His Comforter will comfort you and strengthen you, in all situations.

Jesus likened the Holy Spirit to the wind (John 3:8). We cannot see the Spirit, but we can hear God's voice. We can feel His presence. We know He is there.

The Holy Spirit is not a vague force or entity. He is God Himself. When we are filled with Him, He will carry us, as if on a jet stream, on the strong, sure currents of His love.

CHAPTER TWELVE

DEATH

Death Be not Proud

God intended life to be a glorious adventure ("abundant" is how He described it); one that takes us through dark and sometimes scary valleys, then back up to the mountain tops; across dry, lonely terrains and into lush and fertile lands.

But our adventure is sometimes dimmed by a long shadow, cast by a constant cloud. The cloud is dark, full and too often ready to pour out its cold splash of tears onto our lives. The cloud dampens our moods, sometimes scares us, blocks the light and keeps us from enjoying our days. The cloud is what many psychologists call the ultimate fear: death.

Not everyone is *afraid* to die. Age, background, beliefs, health, family, and culture are factors that affect our perception of death. I don't think I'm afraid to die. But I do struggle over fear of a loved one dying. I fear a disease that might linger and kill me. A sudden accident that takes me or someone I love scares me. If we don't fear death itself, most of us have some fear about the process.

Dag Hammarskjold, who served as secretary-general of the United Nations for eight years and died in a plane crash, wrote, "In the last analysis, it is our conception of death which decides our answers to all the questions that life puts to us."

It is that conception and our attitude toward death I would like to discuss.

As Christians we celebrate Christ's victory over death. Often we sing "He is risen!" and find relief and release and joy in the knowledge that yes, Christ did conquer death.

But God never asks us to be dishonest. We don't have to be afraid to admit that death still affects us, even frightens us.

FACE DEATH HONESTLY

Most of us have heard the familiar words of Psalm 23: "Even though I walk through the valley of the shadow of death, I will fear no evil; for You are with me." As

Sherwood Wirt says, "'You are with me' is not hope; it is absolute certainty. It is Biblical faith based on divine revelation and proven realities." But, he continues, such faith does not ignore the blunt truth that we are still hurt and confused. Nor does it disregard our pain and agony.

When C.S. Lewis was mourning the death of his wife, he wrote, "It is hard to have patience with people who say 'There is no death' or 'Death doesn't matter.' There is death. And whatever is matters. And whatever happens has consequences, and it and they are irrevocable and irreversible . . . I look up into the night sky. Is there anything more certain than that in all those vast times and spaces, if I were allowed to search them, I should nowhere find her face, her voice, her touch? She died. She is dead. Is the word so difficult to learn?"

My younger brother, Glenn, and I were just a year apart. One night, on a dark street, a car hit and killed him. Glenn was still such a young man, in his thirties. His death seemed untimely. It hurt us. We miss him. We mourn for what he never experienced, for the times he won't be with us to laugh, to talk, to just enjoy one another's company. There is an irreconcilable void in our family gatherings. I grieve for my parents, for having lost a son, for myself for having lost a brother, for my other brother Gregg, who is Glenn's twin.

Waves of grief come and go, and can't be escaped. Knowing that Glenn is with the Lord brings immeasurable comfort. But when the waves hit, I understand the cries of the man who wrote, "all your waves and breakers have swept over me" (Psalm 42:7). Death takes us through deep waters and dark, shadowy valleys. Death is a thief and a robber. It takes from us the very thing God bestowed upon us – life. It is a reality we must come face to face with. There is no getting around the tragedy that is death.

A NEW PERSPECTIVE

For centuries people believed that the earth was stationary and the sun moved around it, making the human race the center of the universe. In 1543, Copernicus published a controversial book asserting that the earth and other planets circled around the sun. His ideas changed everyone's perspective on the nature of the universe.

This is what Jesus Christ did to the world's perception of death. He turned it upside down!

Our sins will not allow us to live forever in God's Kingdom ("For the wages of sin is death"). Without the promise of eternal life, death is indeed something to fear. But when Jesus died for our sins, taking them all upon Himself, then rose again on the third day, He proved that eternal life is a reality. Death had been conquered! The robber had been robbed. Life was taken back the day Jesus rose from the dead!

So why do we still have to endure the death process?

PART OF THE JOURNEY

"Strangers and pilgrims on the earth." That's how the Scriptures describe the faithful. "They seek a home-land . . . they desire a heavenly country" (Hebrews 11:13-16).

Though we are strangers and pilgrims, we haven't been left to wander through life without direction. God gave us His Word and He sent His Son Jesus as an example to us of how a man should live.

In His life Jesus included time for friends, for fellowship, for teaching and ministering, for work and for fun. But He also lived with suffering, trials, hardship, heartache, and sorrow. He lived the whole gamut of life to show us what is possible. The end results all turned on His moment of death, when He took upon Himself our sins and defied the powers of evil to prove to us what His love can do. But He didn't stop there!

Three days after His death, He was gloriously and supernaturally resurrected.

Likewise, He asks us to follow Him, and to trust Him through our joys and sorrows, and when we come to the moment of death, to remember His triumph and His victory.

Death is also the great leveler. It is the moment when all people are equal and earthly accomplishments pale. Dr. Maurice S. Rawlings, author of *Beyond Death's Door*, says, "The most significant moment in life is death."

Impending death can cause even the most self-assured soul to re-examine his life.

An old book by M.C. Pritchard titled *Pebbles from the Brink*, published in 1913, recounts many deathbed reflections of well-known thinkers.

Sir Isaac Newton, shortly before his death in 1727 wrote:

"I do not know what I may appear to the world, but to myself I seem to have been only like a boy playing on the seashore, and diverting himself now and then finding a smooth pebble or a prettier shell than ordinary, while the great ocean of truth lies all undiscovered beyond me."

Samuel Johnston proclaimed, "Believe a dying man. Nothing but salvation in Christ can comfort you when you come to die."[3]

CHAPTER ONE

I love what the apostle Paul wrote when the realization of the resurrection hit him.

"Flesh and blood cannot inherit the kingdom of heaven," he said (1 Corinthians 15:50). We can't move into a perfect realm in our present state of being. Our corruptible bodies have to move into an incorruptible state. Our mortal lives have to be transformed into immortality to pass from this life into the next.

---

3   M.C. Pritchard, *Pebbles from the Brink*, (Ottawa: Holiness Movement Print, 1913).

Then, Paul says (and you can almost hear the excitement in his voice), "Death shall be swallowed up in victory!" He went on to cry exultantly, "O death where is thy sting? O grave where is thy victory?"

The purpose for Jesus' death was clear now! Paul understood. He couldn't wait to tell his fellow believers. It really is good news!

And so it should be to us as well when we come to know Jesus and the power of His resurrection. This life is truly a short journey, merely preparing the way for something greater. If we can just get that idea into our hearts and minds, it will change our whole perspective on life! George McDonald wrote, "If you knew what He knows about death, you would clap your listless hands."

I don't know if anyone has ever described the transition from this life to the next better than C.S. Lewis in the closing paragraphs of his *Chronicles of Narnia*.

Aslan the lion, who symbolizes Jesus, has just told the children in the story that they have been in a railway accident. "Your father and mother and all of you are – as you used to call it in the Shadow-Lands – dead . . . . The dream has ended; this is morning."

Lewis writes, "For them it was only the beginning of the real story. All their life in this world . . . had only been the cover and title page; now at last they were beginning Chapter One of the Great Story, which no one on earth has read; which goes on forever; in which every chapter is better than the one before."[4]

Jesus taught us, "I am the way, the truth and the life." He also said, "I am the light of the world."

He is the way – the only way – to heaven. He is the truth that exposes death as a powerless, defeated enemy. He is the light that can push away the clouds.

In Him we are free of all fear, anxiety, worry. In Him we find the hope of peace that passes all understanding. In Him we find the strength to keep our minds fixed on the good things of the Lord.

In Him we will truly live.

---

4   C.S. Lewis, *The Last Battle*, (The Macmillan Co., 1956).

If you have any questions about the Christian life,
if you have recently accepted Jesus Christ as your Savior,
or if we can be of any help to you in your Christian walk,
please write to us in care of:

Maranatha Press
10752 Coastwood Road San Diego, CA 92127
email: itw@maranathachapel.org

It will be our privilege to serve you in this manner.
God bless you.